First World War
and Army of Occupation
War Diary
France, Belgium and Germany

41 DIVISION
Divisional Troops
13 Belgium Field Artillery
1 January 1917 - 17 May 1917

WO95/2625/7

Published by

The Naval & Military Press Ltd

Unit 10 Ridgewood Industrial Park,

Uckfield, East Sussex,

TN22 5QE England

Tel: +44 (0) 1825 749494

www.naval-military-press.com

www.nmarchive.com

This diary has been reprinted in facsimile from the original. Any imperfections are inevitably reproduced and the quality may fall short of modern type and cartographic standards.

© Crown Copyright
Images reproduced by permission of The National Archives, London, England, 2015.

Contents

Document type	Place/Title	Date From	Date To
Heading	WO95/2625/9 41 Div 13 Belgium FA Jan-May 1917		
Heading	41st Division 13th Belgian Fld Arty Jan-May 1917		
Heading	War Diary for January 1917 Of 13th Belgian Field Artillery. Vol 23		
War Diary		01/01/1917	25/01/1917
War Diary		31/01/1917	25/02/1917
Miscellaneous	D.A.G. 3rd Echelon.	28/02/1917	28/02/1917
Heading	War Diary of 13th Belgian Field Artillery for February 1917 Vol 24		
War Diary		01/02/1917	28/02/1917
War Diary		01/02/1917	25/02/1917
Miscellaneous	D.A.G. 3rd Echelon.	01/04/1917	01/04/1917
Heading	War Diary of 13th Belgian Field Artillery for March 1917 Vol 25		
War Diary		01/03/1917	31/03/1917
Miscellaneous	D.A.G. 3rd Echelon.	01/05/1917	01/05/1917
Heading	War Diary for April 1917 of 13th Belgian Field Artillery. Vol 26		
War Diary		01/04/1917	30/04/1917
Miscellaneous	D.A.G. 3rd Echelon.	17/05/1917	17/05/1917
Heading	War Diary for May (1st to 17th) 1917 of 13th Belgian Field Artillery. Attd 2nd Army. Vol 27		
War Diary		01/05/1917	17/05/1917
Heading	41st Division 41st Divl Ammn Column RFA May 1916-Oct 1917 Mar 1918-1919 Sep In Italy 1917 Nov To 1918 Feb 2625		

WO95/2025/9
4 DIV
13 BELGIUM FA
JAN - MAM 1917

41ST DIVISION

13TH BELGIAN FLD ARTY
JAN - MAY 1917

41ST DIVISION

War Diary for January 1917.
of 13" Belgian Field Artillery.

Army Form C. 2118.

141

WAR DIARY
or
INTELLIGENCE SUMMARY.
(Erase heading not required.)

Instructions regarding War Diaries and Intelligence Summaries are contained in F. S. Regs., Part II. and the Staff Manual respectively. Title pages will be prepared in manuscript.

Place	Date	Hour	Summary of Events and Information	Remarks and references to Appendices
	1917 Jan 1		Regiment allotted for administration to H.1st Division.	
			Positions :– 1st Group H.Q. H28 a 2.0.	Wagon-Lines:–
			1st Bty. N4 6½ 2.8	C29 b 4.1
			2nd " H34 c 5.3 (Emplacement N.H.81.05)	N6 b 2.1
			3rd " H34 b 1.7	N6 b 2.5
			Covering from VIERSTRAAT R² (N18 b 2.3) to RUINED FARM (O3 c 8.4)	
			Under tactical command of C.R.A. H.1st Division.	
			Positions :– 2nd Group H.Q. BELGIAN CHATEAU (H23 b 6.6)	Wagon-Lines
			4 Bty. H24 c 8.3	H25 d 9.0
			5 " (one section) H24 b 6.3	H25 c 6.6.
			6 " H24 c 8.8	H25 c 1.9.
			Covering from RUINED FARM (O3 c 8.4) to HILL 60. Under tactical command of C.R.A. H.7th Division.	
	10/11		Owing to re-distribution of sectors C.R.A. H7 Div. ordered one section of 6 Bty. to reserve in wagon-lines.	
	2.5		Severe bombardment of 3rd Bty damaged two guns which were withdrawn & sent for repairs to Base.	

Army Form C. 2118.

1 H 2

WAR DIARY
or
INTELLIGENCE SUMMARY.
(Erase heading not required.)

Instructions regarding War Diaries and Intelligence Summaries are contained in F. S. Regs., Part II. and the Staff Manual respectively. Title pages will be prepared in manuscript.

Place	Date 1917 Jan.	Hour	Summary of Events and Information	Remarks and references to Appendices
	31		back in tent positions. Regimental Hd. M3C22. Troops refused to Belgium Sheet 28 /Hognon	
			Casualties during month.	
	12		Sergeant TAKEN. E. wounded. Died 14/1/17.	
	1		Gr MAKAR A. /	
	1		Gr MAKAR P. /	
	8		Sergeant HOUPPERMAN P.E. /	
	1		Gr LAMBINET A. /	
	1		Gr BRAKEVA G. /	
	19		Gr TITECA H. /	
	21		Gr GUILLAUME N. /	
	24		Sergeant OPDEBEEK C. /	
	25		Gr COQUETTE F. /	
	1		Gr KEYBERGH J. /	
	1		Gr CUYPERS JR /	
	1		Gr BOEL P. /	
	1		2d Lieut. CLAES Louis. /	

Nullpart Avril 1. 1917
Lieuten Officer
13 E Belgian Field Artillery

2353 Wt. W2514/1454 700,000 5/15 D. D. & L. A.D.S.S./Forms/C. 2118.

Ba.13

D.A.G.
3rd Echelon,

Please find herewith War Diary of this unit for February 1917 — also duplicate copies for October, November & December 1916.

Noëlwood
(Liaison Officer) Lieut. R.A.
for O.C. 13th Belgian Field Artillery

28/2/17.

46

Army Form C. 2118.

Vol 24

WAR DIARY
or
INTELLIGENCE SUMMARY.
(Erase heading not required.)

War Diary of 15th Belgian Field Artillery for February 1917.

Maitland
Lieut. R.a.
Liaison Officer.

Army Form C. 2118.

143

WAR DIARY
or
INTELLIGENCE SUMMARY

(Erase heading not required.)

Place	Date	Hour	Summary of Events and Information	Remarks and references to Appendices
	1917 Feb. 1			
	18		Regiment attached for administration to 41st Division.—	
			Positions:— 1st Group H.Q. H25a.2.0	Wagon-lines.
			1st Bty. NH.602.8	G29.d.7.7
			2nd — H34C5.3 (replacement NH.61.0½)	M62.9.7
			3rd — H34.B.17	M62.2.5
			Covering from PIERSTRAAT R.2 (N18.d.2.3) to RUINED FARM (O3c.8.4)	
			under tactical command of C.R.A. 41st Division.	
			Positions:— 2nd Group H.Q. BELGIAN CHATEAU (H23.d.6.6)	Wagon-lines.
			4th Bty. H24.C.8.3	H25.d.9.0
			5th — H24.R.6.3	H26.C.6.6
			6th — H24.C.8.8	H26.C.1.9
			Covering from RUINEDFARM (O3c.8.4) to H.122.60, under tactical command	
			of C.R.A. 47th Division.	
	28		3rd of 1st Group modified by order of C.R.A. 41st Div. to cover from O7b.95.70 to cause.	
			Units in same positions.	
			Regimental H.Q. M3C2.2. Maps referred to Belgium Sheet 28. Ypres & French maps.	

Army Form C. 2118.

144.

WAR DIARY
or
INTELLIGENCE SUMMARY.

(Erase heading not required.)

Instructions regarding War Diaries and Intelligence Summaries are contained in F. S. Regs., Part II. and the Staff Manual respectively. Title pages will be prepared in manuscript.

Place	Date 1917	Hour	Summary of Events and Information	Remarks and references to Appendices
			Casualties during February.	
	Feb. 1		Cn¹ RUYTJENS. P. wounded	
	14		Bar MEYNEN. H. "	
	25		" DENEEF N. "	
	25		Cn¹ VAN CAUWENBERGH. P. "	

Neilcroof
Lieut. R.A.
Liaison Officer
13th Belgian Field Artillery.

2353 Wt. W2344/1454 700,000 5/15 D, D. & L. A.D.S.S./Forms/C. 2118.

Ba 14

D.A.G.
   3rd Echelon.

Please find herewith War Diary of this unit for March 1917.

          Hoellwood
(Liaison Officer) Lieut. R.A.
for O.C. 13th Belgian Field Artillery

1/4/17.

Army Form C. 2118.

WAR DIARY
or
INTELLIGENCE SUMMARY.
(Erase heading not required.)

Vol 25

War Diary of 13th Belgian Field Artillery for March 1917.

Kethlyd
Lieut Co.
Liaison Officer.

Army Form C. 2118.

145.

WAR DIARY
or
INTELLIGENCE SUMMARY.
(Erase heading not required.)

Instructions regarding War Diaries and Intelligence Summaries are contained in F. S. Regs., Part II. and the Staff Manual respectively. Title pages will be prepared in manuscript.

Place	Date 1917	Hour	Summary of Events and Information	Remarks and references to Appendices
	March 1.		Regiment attached for administration to 41st Division.	
			Position – 1st Group HQ. H28a20	Wagon lines
			1st Bty N14 b67.8	C29 b77
			2nd " H34 c5.3 (emplacement at N4 b10.2)	M6 c 7.7
			3rd " H34 b17	M6 b2.5
			Covering from O7 b 95. 70 to 6 canal	
			Under tactical command of C.R.A. 41st Division	
			Position :– 2nd Group HQ Belgian Chateau (H23 b6.6)	Wagon lines
			4 Bty H24 c8.3	H23 d 9.0
			5 " H24 b6.5	H25 c 6.6
			6 " H24 c8.8	H26 c 1.9
			Covers from Ruined Farm (03c04) to Hill 60. Under tactical	
			command of C.R.A. 47th Division.	
	5/9		By orders of R.A. X Corps, 447th Div. Arty, 2nd Group was withdrawn to rest in	
			Steenvoorde area. Battery positions left unoccupied.	
	19		In compliance with orders from Belgian G.H.Q. and after having informed	

Army Form C. 2118.

146.

WAR DIARY
or
INTELLIGENCE SUMMARY.
(Erase heading not required.)

Place	Date 1917 March	Hour	Summary of Events and Information	Remarks and references to Appendices
	19		G.O.C.R.A. X Corps, the Group H.A. and 3 batteries of 2nd Group were interviewed at MAYENBURG (2 miles E. of ROUSBRUGGE) for E.V. (Seine-Inférieure) the Belgian artillery Instruction centre, for Re-armament with a 105 m/m gun. Units of 1st Group in same position. Regimental H.A. M 30.2.2. map referred to Belgium Sheet 28 K/5000, & 10 cl Maps.	
	31		Casualties during March. Nil.	

Neil Vezand
Lieut. R.a.
Liason Officer.
13° Belgian Field Artillery.

15.

D.A.C.
    3rd Echelon.

Herewith please find War
Diary of this Unit for April
1917.

                    Maillyard
                        Lieut R.A.
        Liaison Officer
    13th Belgian Field Artillery

1 5/17.

Army Form C. 2118.

WAR DIARY
or
INTELLIGENCE SUMMARY.
(Erase heading not required.)

War Diary for April 1917 of
13th Belgian Field Artillery.

Army Form C. 2118.

WAR DIARY
or
INTELLIGENCE SUMMARY.
(Erase heading not required.)

146.

Place	Date	Hour	Summary of Events and Information	Remarks and references to Appendices
	1917 April 1		Regiment attached for administration to 41st Division. — Positions:— 1st Group H.Q. H28a2.0 Wagon Lines 1st Battery N4b0½.8 G29 b 7 1 2nd " H34 c5.5 (emplacement in ruins) M 6 b 6 9 1 3rd " H34 b 1 7 M 6 b 2 5	
			Covering Zone 07 F 95.10 to canal. Under tactical command of C.R.A. 41st Div. 3rd Battery moved (guns & a forward emplacement at N4 a 5.8 covering June Canal. 2nd Group (H.Q. & 3 batteries) at Eu (Seine-Inférieure) re-arming with 105 m/m guns. Units of 1st Group in same positions. Regimental H.Q. M3C2.2. Regt referred to Belgian Shel-Zetigen & Trench-Hupe.	
	30		Casualties during April Nil.	Noel Wood Lieut R.A. Liaison Officer. 13e Belgian Field Artillery.

D.A.G.
3rd Echelon.

Please find herewith War Diary of this unit for May 1917. (1st to 17th) also duplicate copies for January, February, March, April and May 1917.

Noëllsyd
Lieut. R.A.
Liaison Officer
17th May '17 for O.C. 13th Belgian Field Artillery

Army Form C. 2118.

WAR DIARY
or
INTELLIGENCE SUMMARY

(Erase heading not required.)

13 Belgian Field Art.

Vol 27

War Diary for May (1st to 14th) 1919
of 13th Belgian Field Artillery. att 2nd Army.

MacLloyd
Lieut. R.e.
Liaison officer.

WAR DIARY
or
INTELLIGENCE SUMMARY

Army Form C. 2118.

Place	Date 1917	Hour	Summary of Events and Information	Remarks and references to Appendices
	May 1		Regiment attached for administration to 41st Division having its Position 1st Group. Ha. H.28.a.2.0. H.Q. H.Q. 1st Bty NH.C.6½.8 G29.b.4.7 2nd " H34.c.53 (1gun NH.t.10.6) N6.29.7 3rd " H34.b.1.7 (1gun NH.a.5.8) N.6.b.2.5	
	14/15 15/16		Orders from O.495.70 to C.H.A.R. under tactical command of the 41st Div. In compliance with G.O.C. R.A.'s orders (R.A. & Byps A.236/25 of 6/5/17) the three remaining batteries of the regiment were relieved by 156 gun batt. of 41st Div (A.190.R.9.A.) and the 5th Bty. A.9.A., in three positions in rear of departure of regiment 1st Group (3 batts. & H.Q.) entrain at HAZENBURG Belgian Railhead (near ROUSBRUGGE) for E.U. (SOMME) for re-armament (with 105 m/m Guns. The regiment having been ordered by Belgian G.H.Q. (O.I.A. of 4th May 1917 para 4.) to rejoin Belgian Army by May 19th 1917. Regimental Hd. N.3C.2.2.	
	17		Kings referred to Belgian Gds hat 28 Lyons & Trench Mops. Casualties during May. 5.5.17. Killed: Gro SABLON A., CORELIERS J., ROBERT J. 5.5.17. Wounded: Gro D'HUESTERS A., BLOCK L., VANDENBERGHE B. MacIlfred Liaison officer, with R.A. 13 F Belgian Field Artillery.	

41ST DIVISION

41ST DIVL AMMN COLUMN RFA

MAY 1916 - ~~DEC 1918~~ OCT 1917

MAR 1918 — 1919 SEP

IN ITALY   1917 NOV TO 1918 FEB

2625

41ST DIVISION

www.ingramcontent.com/pod-product-compliance
Lightning Source LLC
Chambersburg PA
CBHW081252170426
43191CB00037B/2125